A victory is not the destruction in a given area of the insurgent's forces and his political organization. ... A victory is that plus the permanent isolation of the insurgent from the population, isolation not enforced upon the population, but maintained by and with the population.

—David Galula, *Counterinsurgency Warfare; Theory and Practice*

INTRODUCTION

Mao's Tse Tung and his role in the Chinese Revolutionary war is a powerful case study on how a grass roots organization could rise up and defeat a more powerful and established government. Tremendously outnumbered, out-resourced, and oftentimes near the brink of being destroyed, Mao and his Chinese Communist Party (CCP) always found a way to survive. Historians have done a fine job of capturing the many reasons why Mao was successful and the many reasons why the incumbent government was not. But many of these scholars and historians disagree regarding the fundamental principles that Mao employed over a 30 year period to defeat his stronger foe. Some claim that Mao's success was due to a weak central government that was not capable of providing services and good governance outside of its major cities. Others expand upon the previous point by claiming that because the government was not effective outside the urban areas, the larger population density was disenchanted and desired change. Others claim that the sprawling landscape of China was the source of Mao's success because the CCP could seek asylum in the hinterlands. Regardless of what some scholars assert was the source of Mao's success, it must be identified that in most theories the common denominator for success was the population. The population that sought change was overwhelmingly rural and lived outside of China's modern cities. It was this population that Mao was able to influence and use to ultimately defeat the incumbent government.

For the past twelve plus years the US Army has found itself involved in a conflict against an enemy within a country that also has a weak central government which is ineffective outside of

1

its major cities. This is also an enemy that lives amongst a population that feels disenchanted with its government and, like the Maoist rebels, has accessibility to sprawling hinterlands and mountain passes. Similarly, while engaged in this conflict, the US Army has only achieved moderate success gaining the support of the population.

Over this twelve-year period the US Army has implemented several different strategic and tactical approaches in order to defeat this deeply rooted, well-supported insurgency. Because of these different approaches, the US Army has seen its counter-insurgency doctrine evolve in order to capture the lessons learned. Naturally, many of the principles that support the current US Army's counter-insurgency theory are products of past counter-insurgencies but a lot of the newly evolved doctrine has been captured from lessons learned and tactics that worked.

As US political leaders look to end the longest war in its history, there will be a lot of reflection on how the military organizations executed its counter-insurgency operations. Many of these lessons learned will be captured and codified in future counter-insurgency doctrine. Of the many lessons learned from these conflicts, the two fundamental lessons learned by the US Army while combating insurgencies in Iraq and Afghanistan are that no two insurgencies are the same and that the support of the population is necessary for success. The success of Mao and the CCP during their Revolutionary War further demonstrates the importance of the population support. Mao and the CCP were very successful in gaining the support of the population through their influence activities and these lessons are transportable to future United States counterinsurgency efforts.

This research will address the following questions in order to ascertain why Mao was so successful and if these lessons in insurgency can be applied when conducting a successful counterinsurgency campaign. The three pertinent research questions regarding Mao's success can be answered by addressing the why, how, and what. The first two questions that will be addressed are why was Mao successful regarding the support of the population and how was he

2

able to defeat the larger conventional and better trained and resourced force. The third and last question that this paper will answer is what can be learned and captured for use against future insurgencies.

METHODOLOGY

This monograph will attempt to answer these questions through a historical analysis of key events during the Chinese Civil War between the period of 1921-1934. The research will consist of both primary and secondary English sources that focuses on the tactics employed by the CCP during this period. The findings in the historical case study will be summarized and compared to how the US Army conducted operations that were directed at gaining the support of the population during their operations in Afghanistan and Iraq. Prior to the compare and contrast portion of the paper it will be necessary to provide very brief but important background information on China and it will also be necessary to address and define how the US Army conducts influence operations.

The monograph will start with the background context and will address the government, geography, and social aspects of China prior to and during the early stages of the Chinese revolution. This section will highlight key events during the Qing Dynasty during the 1800s and address many of the elements that faced the Qing Dynasty leading up to their demise in 1911. Additionally, this section will also provide a brief topographical and human geography breakdown in order to establish an understanding of the difficulty of governing outside the urban areas during this time period. Finally, this section will define the different class structures that were relevant in the 19th and 20th century and address key relationships between social classes. The overall purpose of this section is to establish a baseline understanding of the conditions prior to the Chinese Revolution and provide a framework in which the rest of this monograph will use

3

to highlight supporting evidence regarding the relationship between Mao's execution of his insurgency and its relation to the population.

In order to identify the "what" of the research question it will be necessary to define and analyze how the US Army employs its counter-insurgency (COIN) operations. The second section of this monograph will set the backdrop by identifying how the US Army defines and executes activities aimed at influencing populations. This section will trace the origins of the US Army's counterinsurgency (COIN) doctrine and then address the evolution of Army doctrine that has been in place over the last 8 to 10 years.

The purpose of the third section is to analyze and assess the current methods in which the US militaryuses regarding population centric warfare. This section will identify the capabilities and core competencies that are outlined in current US Army doctrine which address gaining the support of the population. Additionally, this section will identify some of the tactical employment of influence activities and then finally this section will conclude with an overall assessment regarding the effectiveness in which the US Army executed their Inform and Influence activities during the recent conflicts.

The fourth section of this monograph will be an analysis of the Chinese revolutionary war through the lens of the CCP with a focus on the tactics and techniques that Mao used to gain the support of the population. This section will address Mao's influence approach in order to gain and maintain the support of the population; a support that would be a key element in victory over the KMT. This section will briefly provide a historical backdrop that will address a key period from 1921-1927; the inception of the CCP and its split from traditional Communist thought. This section will also describe the larger framework in which Mao and the CCP would conduct their protracted war and finally this section will conclude with the development and dissemination of Mao's themes and messages used during this period.

The final section of this paper will be the summation of the research conducted. This section will also serve as a means to compare and contrast similarities between implemented tactics between section III and IV. The final portion of this section and this paper will be to provide insight and recommendations into what lessons, if any, the US Army could have taken away from Mao's ability to achieve the support of the population.

HISTORICAL BACKGROUND

The purpose of this section is to establish a baseline understanding of the conditions related to the Chinese government, its geographical characteristics, and its cultural situation during the 19th century and the turn of the 20th century. Many scholars would blame the weakening of the central Chinese government on the interference of the west and their expansionist ideology but the conditions for change in China were put in motion decades before the West arrived.

Government

The Chinese revolution was a process of change and upheaval that has roots stretching back over a century of Chinese history.[1] The origins of change lay in the inability of the old order to handle the population growth outside the urban centers. Many scholars believed that change in China was a part of a natural order process and was only a matter of time that an organization seized the opportunity to replace the current government.[2]

---

[1]Zedong Mao, Stuart R. Schram, and Nancy Jane. Hodes, *Mao's Road to Power: Revolutionary Writings 1912-1949* (Armonk, NY: M.E. Sharpe, 1992), xv.

[2]Lucien Bianco and Muriel Bell, *Origins of the Chinese Revolution* (Stanford, CA: Stanford University Press, 1971), 10.

Long before the turn of the 20th century China had already experienced many crises. Though debatable, it could be said that the decline of the dynastic China started with the arrival of Western powers in 1839 and ended with the 1911 revolution that brought an end to the Qing dynasty.[3] Between these two events China experienced rebellion in the form of the Hundred Days' Reform, the Boxer Rebellion, the first Sino-Japanese War and the Battle of the Concessions, which are also classic landmarks of the crisis that faced the Chinese empire during this time.[4]

In this period of turmoil, the government responsible for leading China was the Qing Dynasty. The Qing Dynasty rose to power in 1644 and led China all the way until the revolution of 1911. The two elements that led the Qing dynastic decline were internal and external forces. Internally, the Qing government was strained to meet the demands of a population that nearly tripled in size during their reign. Unable to provide basic life supporting governmental functions like food and security put the Qing dynasty on notice. Externally during this period the Qing dynasty faced an encroaching western incursion that would be the basis of two wars and a decline in public confidence in the Qing's ability to govern. Unequal treaties that only benefited the western foreigners and an encroachment on the Chinese culture and way of life were a few of the many reasons why the Qing Dynasty were deemed unfit.

Another area in which the Qing Dynasty came up short was their inability to keep pace regarding modernization. During this period China's neighbors Russia and Japan were considered examples of societies that were modernizing their countries in order to keep pace with western competition. Falling behind economically and a need socially for an identity were not the only reasons why China and the Qing Dynasty failed their population. China's government

---

[3]June M. Grasso, Jay P. Corrin, and Michael Kort, *Modernization and Revolution in China* (Armonk, NY: M.E. Sharpe, 1991),25.

[4]Lucien Bianco and Muriel Bell, *Origins of the Chinese Revolution* (Stanford, CA: Stanford University Press, 1971),10.

also failed to modernize their education and military systems, ultimately leaving the door open for several invasions from a foreign army. When combined, the external and internal forces would ultimately be the catalyst for revolution and change in China.

Geography

In order to understand the reason why the conditions were perfect for change in China during the 19th and 20th century it is imperative to understand the impact of the geographical and human terrain of the country. China is a country that stretches some 5000 kilometers (3100 miles) across the central Asian landmass. It is the third largest country behind Russia and Canada and, at the turn of the 20th century, China boasted the world's second largest population at approximately four hundred million people (Europe was first).[5]

The topographical configuration of China can simply be classified as broad plains, expansive deserts, lofty mountain ranges, and vast areas of inhospitable terrain.[6] Additionally, China's large land mass has also been broken down into five distinct homogeneous regions: Eastern China (subdivided into the northeast plain, north plain, and southern hills), Xinjiang-Mongolia, and the Tibetan-highlands.[7] Of the regions mentioned above the eastern and southern half of the country, are the regions that consist of fertile lowlands and foothills producing most of the agricultural output and human population, which explains why this part of China holds the majority of the country's population.[8]

---

[5]Brian Hook and Denis Crispin Twitchett, *The Cambridge Encyclopedia of China* (Cambridge: Cambridge University Press, 1991), 25.

[6]Bruce A. Elleman and S. C. M. Paine, *Modern China: Continuity and Change 1644 to the Present* (Upper Saddle River, NJ: Prentice Hall, 2010), 26.

[7]"CIA World Factbook," CIA World Factbook, http://geography.about.com/library/cia/blcindex.htm, (accessed November 6, 2013).

[8]Brian Hook and Denis Crispin Twitchett, *The Cambridge Encyclopedia of China* (Cambridge: Cambridge University Press, 1991), 52.

China's human terrain has always been and continues to be very complex. The People's Republic of China (PRC) officially recognizes 56 distinct ethnic groups, the largest of which are Han.[9] Though the aggregate numbers were significantly lower during the 1800s, the ratio regarding ethic groups has relatively remained constant. Though very difficult to find scientific data regarding population density during this period, it would be safe to assume that areas around China's population centers and along the Yellow and Yangtze River systems were highly dense.

In order to simplify the Chinese human landscape in the 1800s, one could break it down into three anthropological branches. Five percent of the population consisted of the hill tribes, people located in southwestern China. Fifteen percent were the modernized urbanites that occupied the majority of the cities, and the final eighty percent were the peasant-villagers-farmers who lived on the arable Chinese land.[10] When you combine both the geographic and human terrain onto a single landscape you get a complex picture regarding the difficulty of control in the regions outside the cities.

Social Classes

The social stratification of China during the 19th century can be categorized into four groups: the scholars, farmers, artisans, and tradesmen.[11] Even though there were four distinct social classes the ability to move up and down the social class ladder was not restricted or uncommon. Wealth was also not an enabler to move through the social classes; rather the best means to rise through the social stratification was with government-approved education.

---

[9] Brian Hook and Denis Crispin Twitchett, *The Cambridge Encyclopedia of China* (Cambridge: Cambridge University Press, 1991), 52.

[10]Earl Herbert. Cressy, *Understanding China; a Handbook of Background Information on Changing China* (New York: Nelson, 1957), 26.

[11]Immanuel C. Y. Hsü, *The Rise of Modern China* (New York: Oxford University Press, 1970), 95.

The scholar class, otherwise known as the scholar-gentry, occupied the top levels of the social stratum. The majority of those in this social class were required to pass a governmental examination that eventually gained them access to higher education and a degree. All 27,000 official positions available during the Ch'ing period belonged to those with degrees and were dubbed "official gentry."[12] The second class inside this spectrum did not hold an official position but would be placed in an intermediate class that would not serve in a bureaucratic capacity.

The next social class were the farmers. The farmers' class comprised eighty to ninety percent of the Chinese population in the 19th century. Their significant numbers would play an important role in China for this class was not only responsible for providing all the food for the Chinese people but the taxes placed on this group would be the majority of income for China and its ruling party. The class consisted mainly of peasants who were subjected to many hardships placed on them.

The next class of citizen were the artisans. This group consisted of skilled workers that specialized in carpentry, masonry, ironsmiths, coppersmiths, and tailors to name a few. This class of individual would typically form guilds according to their respective trade. These guilds would serve as the basis in which these artisans would standardize prices and quality of craftsmanship.

At the bottom of the social class were the merchants. This class was not only comprised of the local shop keepers and trade merchants but was also home to many wealthy monopolists traders who controlled the distribution of these commodities from the previous two classes. It is important to understand that wealth was not a requirement to gain entrance into a specific social class.

In addition to the four classes of society during this time, it is important to understand for this paper the dynamic relationship between the peasants in the farmer class and landlords in the merchant class. In the early to mid 1800s eighty percent of the rural population were considered

---

[12]Immanuel C. Y. Hsü, *The Rise of Modern China* (New York: Oxford University Press, 1970), 95.

9

ordinary peasants or farmers. The majority of these peasants not only lacked a formal education, but also were generally illiterate or semi-literate.[13] Many of these peasants, who were never exposed to the ruling class and their prerogatives, relied on the village-and-market center community.[14] These communities would be the basis in which the farmer classes received many of their basic and essential services.

Because government was irrelevant outside the urban areas, the role had to be filled locally. Unfortunately, the role of government during this time was assumed by a group of corrupt and greedy individuals known as the landlords. The landlords were the law at the time and often used brutal tactics to extort money, goods, and services from a poor peasant class; citizens who oftentimes barely had enough money or food to feed their families. Needless to say the relationship between the farmers and the landlords was volatile and full of animosity and this relationship would play a significant role later in the 1920s.

> Throughout its history, the U.S. Army has focused most of its organizational and doctrinal energies preparing for conventional warfare against a similarly armed opponent. Nevertheless, the Army has spent the majority of its time not on the conventional battlefield, but in the performance of myriad operations other than war.
> —Andrew J. Birtle

ORIGINS AND EVOLUTION OF THE FM 3-24

In the well-documented US history of conflict it is easy to see the number of times that the US has fought an insurgency and required the support of the population. One of the first examples of this can be seen in the 1846 Mexican Campaign led by General Winfield Scott. Tremendously undermanned, General Scott would have to assume risk and cut his lines of

---

[13]Denis Crispin. Twitchett and John King Fairbank, *The Cambridge History of China* (Cambridge: Cambridge University Press, 1978), 10.

[14]Ibid.,10.

communications (LOCs) in order to maintain the initiative, threaten Mexico City, and force the Mexican Government to the negotiation table. Understanding that the local population was key to protecting his LOCs, General Scott pacified the urban centers and prevented an insurgency that would have been detrimental to the strength of the force and his ability to conduct future operations. Without the support of the population, General Scott would not have been able to focus on the conventional elements of war and eventually achieve the operational goals and desired political end state.[15]

This section will describe the evolution of the theory of population centric warfare and will highlight the inception of the new US Army doctrine that guides inform and influence activities. In accomplishing this it will be necessary to historically trace and highlight several very important counterinsurgency concepts and the experts whose work on this topic had an impact on the creation of current doctrine.

The recent wars in both Afghanistan and Iraq had a tremendous impact on doctrine and its evolving principles that are still continuously adapting to an enemy and their operational environment. Following the fall of Baghdad and the end of major combat operations in Iraq in 2004, the US Army had to address what could be considered an anomaly, which was the emergence of an insurgency following its extremely successful execution of a high intensity conflict (HIC) during the initial invasion. The doctrine that would evolve as a result of this anomaly was the Army's counterinsurgency publication Field Manual 3-24 (FM 3-24).

FM 3-24 was written in 2006 as a result of the unforeseen insurgency that emerged in Iraq after the fall of Baghdad. This new doctrine would serve as the document to which all commanders would reference regarding the conduct of counterinsurgency operations (COIN). Its introduction to the forces deployed during this period served to fill a 20-year doctrinal gap

---

[15]Timothy D. Johnson, *A Gallant Little Army: The Mexico City Campaign* (Lawrence, KS.: University Press of Kansas, 2007), 210-271.

addressing counterinsurgency operations.[16] All doctrine prior to the creation of FM 3-24 had only addressed those later stages of an insurgency, which focused on defeating an already established guerrilla force.[17] What was unique about FM 3-24 is that it addressed an insurgency from the beginning to the end, providing a Jominian how-to style approach for success.

Since FM 3-24 is a comprehensive guide on how to defeat an insurgency the range of topics discussed extends from the foundations of an insurgency, the dynamics and characteristics of an insurgency, and the tactics associated with the defeating of an insurgency. But the topic of most significance for this paper that is addressed in FM 3-24 is the importance of gaining the support of the host nation populace. The document's introduction states:

> At its heart, a counterinsurgency is an armed struggle for the support of the population. This support can be achieved or lost through information engagement, strong representative government, access to goods and services, fear, or violence. This armed struggle also involves eliminating insurgents who threaten the safety and security of the population. However, military units alone cannot defeat an insurgency.[18]

This was a strong endorsement at the beginning of the doctrine that guided all US Army COIN operations after 2006, but this theory of denying the enemy safe havens within the population is not an original concept. This concept was the product of many different past insurgencies and therefore many theorists recognized the population as the key for defeating an insurgency.

In the book *Understanding Counterinsurgency Doctrine, Operations and Challenges* the lead author of FM 3-24, Conrad Crane, credits noted counterinsurgency experts Frank Kitson and

---

[16]The U.S. Army/Marine Corps Counterinsurgency Field Manual: U.S. Army Field Manual No. 3-24: Marine Corps Warfighting Publication No. 3-33.5 (Chicago: University of Chicago Press, 2007), forward.

[17]Ibid., vii.

[18]The U.S. Army/Marine Corps Counterinsurgency Field Manual: U.S. Army Field Manual No. 3-24: Marine Corps Warfighting Publication No. 3-33.5 (Chicago: University of Chicago Press, 2007), vii.

Roger Trinqueir for providing the initial framework of the document.[19] Both Kitson and

Trinqueir had tremendous experience dealing with an insurgency during their time in the British

and French militaries. But the one theorist that arguably had the most influence during the

development of US Army COIN doctrine was David Galula.

David Galula was an Army officer whose service in the French Army gained him a

wealth of experience and knowledge in the realm of conducting counterinsurgency operations.

During his service, Galula was assigned to China from 1945-1948 and was witness to the events

leading up to the defeat of the incumbent government in China. From 1949-1950 he served in

Greece during their civil war and then from 1956 to 1958 he also served in Algeria.[20] David

Galula's book, *Counterinsurgency Warfare, Theory, and Practice*, was written in 1964 and its

theory and systematic approach to counterinsurgency warfare is still applicable today. Similar to

the principles outlined in FM 3-24, Galula's book is prescriptive in nature and provides a detailed

how-to approach regarding the characteristics, pitfalls and keys to success for defeating an

insurgency.

In his book, Galula takes a unique approach and addresses insurgency warfare from the

lens of the insurgent. The author broadly identifies the characteristics and prerequisites for a

successful insurgency and eventually addresses an insurgency at the strategic and tactical level.

Many times throughout his book Galula makes mention of the importance of the population's

support but doesn't really go into detail until chapter 5. In this chapter the author identifies

several principles that he classifies as laws. It is here that Galula drives home his point about the

necessity of the population support. In this section the author states that "A victory [in a

counterinsurgency] is not the destruction in a given area of the insurgent's forces and his political

---

[19]Thomas Rid and Thomas A. Keaney, Understanding Counterinsurgency: Doctrine, Operations and Challenges (Milton Park, Abingdon, Oxon,: Routledge, 2010), 61.

[20]David Galula, *Counterinsurgency Warfare; Theory and Practice* (New York: Praeger, 1964), 1.

organization. ... A victory is that plus the permanent isolation of the insurgent from the population."[21]

Additionally, Galula mentions that:

> In conventional warfare, strength is assessed according to military or other tangible criteria, such as the number of divisions, the position they hold, the industrial resources, etc. In revolutionary warfare, strength must be assessed by the extent of support from the population as measured in terms of political organization at the grass roots.[22]

Other individuals whose expertise regarding the conduct of executing a counterinsurgency that addresses the importance of the winning the population support are Dr. Bard O'Neill and Sir Robert Grainger Ker Thompson. In his book *Insurgency & Terrorism*, Dr. O'Neill, just as Galula did, dedicates an entire chapter to the topic of population support. In this chapter Dr. O'Neill addresses the types of popular support and offers techniques in which both an insurgent and counterinsurgent can employ in order to gain this advantage. But the most significant endorsement that Dr. O'Neill makes in this chapter states "that in order for an insurgent to offset the superior resources of the incumbent government the insurgent leaders will stress the critical strategic role of popular support", and that "Most insurgent leaders know that they risk destruction by confronting government forces in direct conventional engagements." [23]

Sir Robert Grainger Ker Thompson was a British Military Officer and counterinsurgency expert who has been touted as the leading expert on countering the Mao Tse-tung technique of rural guerrilla insurgency.[24] Thompson impact on the US Army's counterinsurgency and

---

[21]David Galula, *Counterinsurgency Warfare; Theory and Practice* (New York: Praeger, 1964),78.

[22]Ibid.,78.

[23]Bard E. O'Neill, *Insurgency & Terrorism: From Revolution to Apocalypse* (Washington, DC: Potomac Books, 2005), 52.

[24]U.S. Army Information Proponent Office, "Instructor's Guide To Inform And Influence Activities," US Army War College, section goes here, accessed December 19, 2013, http://www.carlisle.army.mil/.

influence doctrine can be found in his book *Defeating Communist Insurgency: the Lessons of Malaya and Vietnam.* In this book Thompson identifies thirteen key elements in his approach to defeating a communist insurgency. All thirteen elements are related to defeating an insurgency but it is the very first element in Thompson's approach that states:

> The people are the key base to be secured and defended rather than territory won enemy bodies counted. Contrary to the focus of conventional warfare, territory gained, or casualty counts are not of overriding importance in counter-guerrilla warfare. The support of the population is the key variable. Since many insurgents rely on the population for recruits, food, shelter, financing, and other materials, the counter-insurgent force must focus its efforts on providing physical and economic security for that population and defending it against insurgent attacks and propaganda.[25]

This principle in Thompson's book, as with O'Neill and Gulula's approach to the population can be viewed as the foundation within the theory that shaped FM 3-24.

In 2006 FM 3-24 was codified as doctrine. The theories and principles that provide the framework for this document are rooted in history but through the natural progression of time the US Army has adapted new principles that builds on previous theory and doctrine. Up until 2010, the US Army housed many of its principles associated with population centric warfare in FM 3-24. This changed when the Army reinvented the manner in which it published doctrine. As recent as 2009 the US Army doctrinal library housed over 625 different forms of publications that provided some form of guidance for all foreseeable types of military operation. The revision and maintenance of this enormous library of documents was cumbersome and often overlooked which was why the US Army sought to revamp its approach regarding the dissemination of doctrine. The Army's 2015 initiative was adopted to replace this system with the intent to capture current theory through doctrine and to establish a baseline of efficiency regarding the upkeep and relevancy of future doctrine.

---

[25]Thomas Rid and Thomas A. Keaney, *Understanding Counterinsurgency: Doctrine, Operations and Challenges* (Milton Park, Abingdon, Oxon,: Routledge, 2010), 59.

During this extreme doctrine makeover the US Army has identified two key publications as the foundation for the future doctrine. Army Doctrine Reference Publication 1 The Army (ADRP1), and Army Doctrine Reference Publication (ADRP) 3-0 Unified Land Operations (ULO), are the two bedrock publications that serve as the basis for all other doctrine. ADRP 3-0 ULO, is the document that attempts to capture many of the lessons learned from the recent wars in Iraq and Afghanistan as well as maintain other key principles that have been proven successful based on implementation.

The central theme for ULO describes how the Army seizes, retains, and exploits the initiative to gain and maintain a position of relative advantage in sustained land operations through simultaneous offensive, defensive, and stability operations in order to prevent or deter conflict, prevail in war, and create the conditions for favorable conflict resolution.[26]

Within ADRP 3-0 there are many principles and lines of effort that are discussed, but for the purposes of this paper the focus will be on how this new doctrine addresses operations designed at influencing a targeted audience or specific population. ADRP 3-0 identifies this line of effort as Inform and Influence Activities (IIA). The primary purpose for IIA is to inform the United States and targeted global audiences, influence foreign audiences, and affect adversary and enemy decision-making.[27]

The relationship between ULO and IIA is complex but also symbiotic in nature. While conducting offensive, defensive, and stability operations during the course of a campaign, commanders should approach inform and influence activities as combat enablers and therefore must employ them as such. A commander has the responsibility to the American public to keep them informed of all operations that are being conducted in a respected battle space; these

---

[26]United States, *Army Doctrine Reference Publication, 3-0, Unified Land Operations*, (Washington DC: Headquarters, Department of the Army, 2013), 1-1.

[27]Ibid., 1-1.

operations are classified inform activities. But a commander has the option to perform very specific missions that are aimed at influencing a foreign audience's perception regarding military conflict taking place in their region. Section four of this monograph will dive into more detail about how the US Army doctrinally performs their influence operations.

Since the turn of the 20th century the most common form of armed conflict has taken the shape of an insurgency. Through either personal experience or research many counterinsurgency experts agree that the heart of any insurgency is found with the support of the population. Military history has captured the numerous times in which a population and its support was essential to the outcome of a conflict. From the American colonist to the British loyalist, from the "zones of protection" established in the Philippines in order to defend against the guerillas, the American military has in some form or fashion had to take into consideration the support of the population. Recent conflict has re-enforced this point even further.

At the strategic level the US Army's approach of "winning the hearts and minds" of the Iraqi and Afghanistan populations is validated through the framework of its COIN and IIA doctrine, but the question remains are the methods that are being employed at the operational and tactical level in line with reality of the environmental conditions?

INFLUENCE ACTIVITIES ON THE MODERN BATTLEFIELD

Gaining the population's support is no longer a novel idea but rather the central theme when executing a counterinsurgency. History provides many examples of this and the creation of FM 3-24 supports this theory within its principles. Mao Tse Tung was very cognizant of the fact that the peasant population would be the key to his success if the CCP were to defeat the Nationalists. But theory alone is not a recipe for success. Mao's ability to effectively influence the population would be found in his employment of influence tactics.

The previous section traced the history and evolution of the US Army's doctrine and also broadly touched upon the basic theory of influence with regards to gaining the population's support. This section will dive deeper into the specifics regarding the core competencies of the US Army's influence tactics and techniques used today. This section will also address the effectiveness of the US Army's doctrine through an analysis of the core competencies regarding influence activities.

FM 3-13, Inform and Influence Activities is the current US Army doctrine that houses the current tactics and according to FM 3-13:

> All inform activities are those activities that coordinate, synchronize, and integrate the information-related capabilities application to accomplish the mission. This is done through the use of information-related capabilities such as public affairs, MISO, civil affairs operations, and others enablers the commander has at their disposal in order to inform foreign audiences and to provide Army support to strategic communication.[28]

The foreign audience in this case would most likely be our allies and other friendly states in and around the theater of operations.

In contrast to inform activities, influence activities are defined as:

> Strictly limited in their scope and their target. The US Army looks to influence foreign audiences with the purpose of persuading specific selected audiences to support the U.S. objectives within the area of operations or to compel those audiences to stop supporting the adversary. They do this through planned operations to convey selected information and indicators to audiences to influence their emotions, motives, objective reasoning, and ultimately the behavior of governments, organizations, groups, and individuals.[29]

The bottom line regarding these two separate lines of operation is their target audience. Inform activities are directed at domestic and friendly audiences where influence activities are targeted at adversarial and non-supporting audiences.

---

[28]United States, *Field Manual 3-13, Inform and Influence Activities* (Washington DC: Headquarters, Department of the Army, 2013), 1-2.

[29]United States Department of Defense, *Joint Publication 1-02 Department of Defense Dictionary of Military and Associated Terms,* (Washington, DC: Government Printing Office, 2006).

It is fundamental to understand that IIA is a staff integration function that provides the commander options regarding information related capabilities. The four enabling capabilities that fall under IIA are MISO (Military Information Support Operations), Public affairs, leader engagements and Combat Camera.[30] Of the four enabling functions of IIA, MISO is considered the core capability that a commander has when they wish to influence a targeted audience.

Prior to 2010, the US Army's primary capability used to influence a target audience was known as Psychological Operations (PSYOP). Post 2010 and in conjunction with the overhaul of doctrine, psychological operations would cease to exist as the proper nomenclature and therefore all influencing activities would fall under the newly minted Military Information Support Operations (MISO) per view. Of note though, the term PYSOP has not been totally removed from the US Army vernacular, because PYSOP now refers to a career management field, military occupational specialty, or branch of the military that supports MISO.[31]

FM 3-53 is the new doctrine that guides all MISO. The doctrine states that the primary purpose of the influence line of effort within MISO is to essentially change the decision-making and behavior of all foreign populations in order to support the operations being conducted.[32] These activities are also directed at the enemy decision makers with the intent to convince or compel them to surrender or malinger, desert, and cease resistance.[33]

The rest of this section will address the MISO core competencies outlined in FM 3-53 while assessing the effectiveness of their recent employment. The core competencies of MISO

---

[30]U.S. Army Information Proponent Office, "Instructor's Guide To Inform And Influence Activities," US Army War College, section goes here, accessed December 19, 2013, http://www.carlisle.army.mil/.

[31]United States, *Field Manual 3-53, Military Information Support Operations* (Washington DC: Headquarters, Department of the Army, 2013), v.

[32]Ibid., 1-10.

[33]United States, *Field Manual 3-53, Military Information Support Operations* (Washington DC: Headquarters, Department of the Army, 2013), v.

include the planning, the development, the delivery, and the assessment of effectiveness. For the purpose of this monograph, the core competencies of theme and message development and delivery will be addressed. The development of themes and messages are devised to ensure the target audiences' understanding and influence their attitudes towards change that reflects a more favorable environment for the US military.[34] FM 3-53 states MISO forces create messages and plan actions to reach selected audiences with the intent to achieve specific cognitive and psychological effects, including behavioral changes. The messages and actions are devised to ensure the TA understanding, and influence their propensity toward a desired behavior change.[35] In order to do this PYSOP Soldiers must:

1) Understand the cognitive and motivating factors of the identified target audiences' behaviors.
2) Understand the environmental conditions, and social, cultural, and historical factors that influence decision-making and subsequent actions.
3) Consider the physical and social needs that motivate the target audiences' behavior.

A way in which the US Army attempts to capture all three points above is through the use of a tool called PMESII-PT. PMESII-PT stands for Political, Military, Economic, Social, Infrastructure, Information, Physical Environment, and Time and is a starting point in which US forces can capture some of the most important elements of a social system. It is important to understand that PMESII-PT by itself provides a limited snapshot of an environment at a given time. In order for the true essence and greatest understanding of an operational environment to be gained, a continuous cycle of learning must be adopted and many experts should be used. FM 3-53 recommends that when developing specific themes and messages for a target audience many experts from the fields of social and behavioral sciences, advertising, cultural anthropology, humanities, language and culture, journalism, media and mass communication, political science,

---

[34]United States, *Field Manual 3-53, Military Information Support Operations* (Washington DC: Headquarters, Department of the Army, 2013), 1-7.

[35]Ibid., 1-7.

public relations and communications, social marketing, statistics, and trend analysis be included in the process.[36] The importance of the consolidation of all these experts is to assist in generating the most accurate, applicable, and effective influence messages.

The RAND National Defense Research Institute, a leading research organization, conducted a study on the effectiveness of the US military's influencing activities in Afghanistan from the time frame of 2001-2010. The research suggests that the effectiveness of the US military's influence methods in Afghanistan, specifically the military messages and themes were missing their intended effect. The study focused on the credibility, appropriate cultural, social, political, or religious context, and the overall effectiveness of the messages and themes developed.[37] Results from the extensive research concluded that the US military's effectiveness received a grade from mixed to ineffective throughout the period of the study. Reasons for this ineffectiveness were blamed on the lack of precision and vagueness of the messages that stemmed from the main themes. Often times the messages targeted the wrong demographic and the message was classified as confusing or lacked cohesion with other strategic messages being employed.[38]

Developing accurate, applicable, and effective messages is just one of the core competencies of MISO. The other core competency that this monograph will address is the delivery mechanism regarding the themes and messages developed. According to FM 3-53, a commander has many options available to him in which to effectively influence a targeted audience. In order to shape the operational environment (OE) MISO forces must conduct a

---

[36]United States, *Field Manual 3-53, Military Information Support Operations* (Washington DC: Headquarters, Department of the Army, 2013), 1-53.

[37]Arturo Munoz, "U.S. Military Information Operations in Afghanistan," : Effectiveness of Psychological Operations 2001-2010, 96 accessed February, 08, 2014, http://www.rand.org/pubs/monographs/MG1060.html.

[38]Ibid., 96.

multitude of different operations. Of these operations the most critical, regarding influencing a

targeted audience, is done through interacting, directly and indirectly, with foreign-friendly,

neutral, adversary, and enemy targeted audiences for persuasive and psychological effect.[39]

FM 3-53 lists that appropriate delivery platforms are to include indigenous, commercial

off-the-shelf and advanced media platforms, such as satellite television and long-range terrestrial

radio, and virtual (web) applications.[40] More specifically the RAND report addresses more of the

operational and tactical level delivery platforms and identifies radio, leaflets and posters,

newspapers and magazine, billboards and face to face engagements as the means in which the

PYSOP message could be delivered.[41]

Without question the US militaryused diverse methods to reach the desired target

audience. But the methods used, whether it be a leaflet, billboard, or newspaper was not as

effective as it could be regarding influencing the population. The RAND report highlights that in

both the Kandahar and Helmand provinces that over 90% of the population owned a radio and

over 61% received their information from the radio. Additionally, of this population

demographic, over 55% listened to the radio daily and had 60% confidence in the message being

broadcasted.[42]

The report also highlights that any print related message often didn't reach its desired

audience for a multitude of reasons. Illiteracy in Afghanistan is extremely high and therefore

getting a written message out was difficult. For those who could read the handbills, posters, and

other print products the message was not often well received because of a stigma associated with

---

[39]United States, *Field Manual 3-53, Military Information Support Operations* (Washington DC: Headquarters, Department of the Army, 2013), 1-4.

[40]Ibid., 1-7.

[41]Arturo Munoz, "U.S. Military Information Operations in Afghanistan," : Effectiveness of Psychological Operations 2001-2010, 96, accessed February, 08, 2014, http://www.rand.org/pubs/monographs/MG1060.html.

[42]Ibid., 97.

the US Military.

The final issue regarding how the US militaryapproached its influence line of effort can be viewed as a supply and demand issue. As mentioned previously, a PYSOP Soldier is the primary means to plan, develop, deliver and assess the messages and themes that are disseminated. It takes a considerable amount of time and education to produce PYSOP Solider. The problem in both Iraq and Afghanistan was simply a numbers game. There were not enough specialized PSYOP Soldiers to execute all the required missions leaving the void to be filled by Soldiers who were not trained properly to effectively disseminate the required messages.[43]

There were many great things done in the realm of influence operations in both Iraq and Afghanistan. The US Army's MISO doctrine 3-53 does a great job of providing a framework in which to develop, disseminate and assess the themes and messages that are directed at a targeted audience. But as evident in the previous paragraph, the US militarywas not as effective as they could have been. The accuracy and applicability in conjunction with a non-personal manner in which the messages were delivered were some of the shortfalls of the US Army's influence activities. The next section will use the same format and describe some methods in which Mao and the CCP developed and disseminated their themes and messages.

CHINESE REVOLUTIONARY WAR CASE STUDY

Revolutionary War Background

The history of the Chinese Civil War is a story of the rise and fall of dynasties and governments, of risk and opportunity taken and lost, and a story of will and determination. But

---

[43] Arturo Munoz, "U.S. Military Information Operations in Afghanistan," : Effectiveness of Psychological Operations 2001-2010, 90, accessed February, 08, 2014, http://www.rand.org/pubs/monographs/MG1060.html.

more evident than anything, the history of the Chinese Civil War is complex and extremely long. The beginning of this section will provide a brief background of the events leading up to the creation of the CCP and then the remainder of the section will focus on the Chinese Civil War and Mao's role in this protracted conflict. The second half of this section will describe the three-phased framework from which Mao would use to guide the activities and the final part of this section will address the techniques Mao used to develop and disseminate his messages and themes in order to influence the population.

The collapse of the Qing dynasty in 1911 was the end of a system that ruled China for thousands of years. The cause of the collapse of the dynastic system and birth of the Republic of China is linked to the Xinhai Revolution, which was a series of revolts and uprisings that were a response to the weak Qing Dynasty's inability to modernize China's infrastructure and also address foreign influence.[44] This revolution would ultimately leave the door open for a new governmental system, which would replace the old imperial way of life.

Following the fall of the Qing Dynasty, the KMT assumed the position of the legitimate governing body for the people of China.[45] One of the key leaders of this party was Chiang Kai-shek who was best described as a revolutionary militarist known for his forceful methods of reuniting the people of China.[46] But even with a new, heavy-handed, non-dynastic government in place, China was still not as stable as it could be. The social and political environment that encompassed China at this time would be the catalyst to what is known as the May Fourth Movement. Though many different thought systems were evoked in an attempt to fill the old

---

[44]Xing Li, *The Rise of China and the Capitalist World Order* (Farnham, England: Ashgate Pub., 2010) 25.

[45]I. F. W. Beckett, *Modern Insurgencies and Counter-insurgencies: Guerrillas and Their Opponents since 1750* (London: Routledge, 2001), 70.

[46]Ibid., 70.

24

intellectual gap created by the fall of the last Chinese dynasty, none seemed to unite the country of China until after the May Fourth Movement.[47]

The May Fourth Movement was a demonstration in protest against the Chinese government's failure to take back land lost to Japan following World War I. The movement was a series of strikes and revolts that would last four years from 1917-1921 and would contribute to the rise of the student and labor movements, the reorganization of the KMT, and most importantly this movement would see the creation of the Chinese Communist Party.[48] Often considered one of the most important and influential movements in Chinese history, the May Fourth Movement would set the conditions for the Chinese political and social landscape for the next thirty years.

Following the May Fourth Movement, the KMT, a growing nationalist movement, would reinvent itself as a political organization and rise to power and assume the role of government for the country. Sun Yat-sen the leader of this nationalist movement saw it necessary to set the conditions for a national renaissance based on disciplined unity, and therefore one of the first orders of business the KMT leadership had was to remove the corrupt warlords who illegally assumed power in the rural areas during China's transitional period.[49]

At the same time that KMT was rising to power the seeds for the communist party were being planted. Influenced by the 1917 Bolshevik revolution in Russia and motivated by the events of the May Fourth Movement, the CCP was founded in 1921 in Shanghai.[50] For about a half-decade and in an attempt to consolidate power in China, the Nationalist and the CCP had

---

[47]Tony Saich and Bingzhang Yang, *The Rise to Power of the Chinese Communist Party: Documents and Analysis* (Armonk, NY: M.E. Sharpe, 1996), xlv.

[48]Cezong Zhou, *The May Fourth Movement: Intellectual Revolution in Modern China* (Cambridge: Harvard University Press, 1960), 2.

[49]I. F. W. Beckett, *Modern Insurgencies and Counter-insurgencies: Guerrillas and Their Opponents since 1750* (London: Routledge, 2001), 70.

[50]Ibid.,70.

joined forces. The Nationalists were based on Marxist-Leninism ideology and therefore sought to unite the rural populations through the establishments of the middle class workers associations and trade unions. Around 1925 the Nationalist and the CCP split. The cause for this split stemmed from the fundamental ideology. Where the nationalist saw the working class as the key to revolution, Mao believed it was the peasantry and therefore when members of the CCP moved to fill the void that was created with the ousting of the rural warlords, the CCP and KMT became at odds with the KMT feeling that the CCP were infringing on Chiang's authoritarianism.[51]

Though not entirely happy with Mao's divergence from the traditional Marxist ideology, the CCP would continue to receive guidance from Moscow. Part of the guidance Mao Tse-Tung and the CCP received would lead to a series of uprisings known as the 'Autumn Harvest'; all of which was met with defeat at the hands of the Nationalist Army. Defeated and without support, Mao sought refuge in the mountainous hinterlands of southern and western China.[52] The fallout from the defeats during the 'Autumn Harvest' was a defining moment for Mao and the CCP. The Russian communist system was based on the industrial proletariat just as Marx had intended, whereas Mao's communist movement in China tended to focus more on the peasant; where Mao naturally felt more comfortable.[53] This difference in ideology was fundamental and would ultimately lead to the division between CCP and Moscow.

The challenges that faced the CCP during the latter part of the 1920s were staggering. For the remainder of the late 1920s into the 1930s Mao and his followers would be forced to conduct their communist activities in undesirable areas far from the reach of the standing government. The CCP strength was not only shattered by the conflict that took place during this

---

[51]I. F. W. Beckett, Modern Insurgencies and Counter-insurgencies: Guerrillas and Their Opponents since 1750 (London: Routledge, 2001), 70.

[52]Ibid.,71.

[53]Samuel B. Griffith, Mao Tse-Tung on Guerrilla Warfare (Praeger Publishers, 1961), 17.

period but it was dispersed across a vast geography as well. In order to escape the continuous assaults from the Nationalist Party and survive, Mao would have to retreat to the forsaken region of China's Jinggangshan, a mountainous region on the border of Jiangxi and the Hunan provinces.[54] It was here that Mao along with 2500 survivors would build his communist church.[55] This place would bear the fruit of the communist seeds that Mao would take forward for the remainder of the conflict.

Mao's Protracted Framework

History highlights that protracted conflict favors the insurgent. Outnumbered and outgunned by the Nationalist Army, Mao would employ his theory known as the 'people's war.' Simply defined, the 'people's war' was a military-political strategy designed to gain and maintain the support of the population. Once the support of the population has been gained Mao and his guerrilla forces would draw the conventional army deep into the interior lines and then systematically bleed the enemy through the use of mobile and guerrilla's tactics.[56] Within this politico-military approach was a three-phased strategy that would be implemented against the nationalist forces. The first phase was the strategic defensive. The second phase was the strategic stalemate and the final phase was the strategic offensive phase.[57]

---

[54]June M. Grasso, Jay P. Corrin, and Michael Kort, *Modernization and Revolution in China* (Armonk, NY: M.E. Sharpe, 1991), 110.

[55]Ibid., 110.

[56]I. F. W. Beckett, *Modern Insurgencies and Counter-insurgencies: Guerrillas and Their Opponents since 1750* (London: Routledge, 2001), 74.

[57]Bard E. O'Neill, *Insurgency & Terrorism: From Revolution to Apocalypse* (Washington, DC: Potomac Books, 2005), 50.

The strategic defense could be considered the pre-revolutionary phase in which Mao and his communist forces would consolidate and organize themselves.[58] A key objective for this phase was to expand the party organization and establish necessary infrastructure for future development of the revolution and eventual movement into phase two of Mao's revolutionary war.[59] This phase is extremely important because this is when the revolutionist sought to plant the seeds regarding popular support. In this phase insurgents used a multitude of subversive techniques to mentally prepare the population to resist the occupying force. These techniques included propaganda, demonstrations, boycotts and sabotage.[60] It is in this phase that Mao looked to consolidate power among the local governments. It was also in this phase that Mao looked to legitimize his cause to the people, while delegitimizing the KMT's ability to perform its core functions as a government. Additionally, throughout this phase Mao suggests that the movement's leadership should focus on recruiting, organizing, and training the cadre members. The infiltrating of key government organizations and the establishment of intelligence operations and support networks are also vital during this phase. Finally, the execution of subversive activities is directed toward the occupying force but major combat is avoided.[61] The purpose of these attacks is to drain the enemy of blood and treasure and to gain legitimacy amongst the population. Success in this phase was critically important for transition into phase two of Mao's strategy.

The second phase, which can be translated as the strategic stalemate phase, naturally picks up where phase one left off. With the conditions set from the first phase, Mao makes the

---

[58]I. F. W. Beckett, Modern Insurgencies and Counter-insurgencies: Guerrillas and Their Opponents since 1750 (London: Routledge, 2001), 74.

[59]Ibid., 74.

[60]United States, Field Manual 3-53, Military Information Support Operations (Washington DC: Headquarters, Department of the Army, 2013),1-6.

[61]Ibid.,1-6.

transition from covert guerrilla attacks to overt attacks on the host nation infrastructure. Additionally, Mao recommends that during this phase an emphasis on subversive activities like clandestine radio broadcasts, newspapers, and pamphlets that openly challenge the control and legitimacy of the established authority are ramped up.[62] The purposes of these inform and influence activities are to further delegitimize the government in the eyes of the population and then use this loss of faith as an opportunity to expand the insurgent base. Finally, it is important to note that focus on recruiting, organizing, and training the cadre members as well as the establishment of more advanced intelligence operations and support networks is still critical in this phase. Transition from phase two to three cannot happen until the insurgent infrastructure and institutions are established, functional, and legitimate. Once parity is perceived regarding resources, manpower, and capabilities to be gained then transition to phase III is possible.

The final and third phase of Mao's Revolutionary war was the strategic offensive phase. This was the phase in which Mao transitions from subversive warfare to a conventional war aimed at destroying the nationalist forces. In addition to the military aspect of this strategy, Mao suggests that during this phase all governmental agencies are destroyed and cease to function. Concurrent to operations, Mao also highlights the need to consolidate and protect all gains that are achieved during this phase and this is to be done through the establishment of an effective civil administration, establishment of an effective military organization, a balanced social and economic development, and the ability to mobilize the populace to support the insurgent organization.[63] The end state of this phase is a total collapse of the incumbent government and its ability to conduct offensive and defensive operations. But it is important to note that victory could be achieved in any of the phases through the progression of the three-phase approach if the

---

[62] United States, Field Manual 3-53, *Military Information Support Operations* (Washington DC: Headquarters, Department of the Army, 2013),1-33.

[63] Ibid., 1-34.

enemy's will has been broken.[64]

The People's War

The previous paragraphs provided the operational framework through which Mao would conduct his protracted 'people's war'. The following pages will be dedicated to dissecting the methods used by Mao in order to influence the population's support during the Chinese Revolutionary War.

Mao understood that the revolution would need lots of time and space in order for the CCP to recruit, equip, and train the forces required to eventually defeat the Nationalist Army on a conventional battlefield. The rural areas away from China's population centers were well outside the reach of the Nationalist ability to influence, therefore making the peasant population an ideal demographic in which Mao could establish a base of constituents and supporters.[65]

Mao Tse-Tung was born in China's southern province of Hunan in the peasant village of Shaoshan.[66] Born to a famer, Mao's early life found his duty to the family farm. As a middle class peasant Mao was exposed to the harsh realities of peasantry life. This exposure would help shape and condition Mao's attitude and values associated with life outside the population centers.

Though Mao parted ways with his family and their peasant lifestyle around the age of 16 he never forgot his roots.[67] Prior to the split of the CCP and KMT, Chiang Kai-shek took command of the National Revolutionary Army and in 1926 Mao was given the task of returning to his home province and starting a revolution based around the peasantry. At this time there

---

[64]Bard E. O'Neill, *Insurgency & Terrorism: From Revolution to Apocalypse* (Washington, DC: Potomac Books, 2005), 53.

[65]Brian Hook and Denis Crispin Twitchett, *The Cambridge Encyclopedia of China* (Cambridge: Cambridge University Press, 1991), 53.

[66]Jonathan Clements, *Mao* (London: Haus Pub., 2006), pg.1.

[67]Ibid., 2.

were approximately 30 million peasants that lived at or below the subsistence level in this area.[68]

Though massive in numbers, the peasant population was extremely decentralized and

unorganized in the rural areas. The lack of a unifying factor and simple geography made the

peasant population a great opportunity for all. Pillaged by tax collectors, robbed by landlords,

harassed by provincial soldiery and slaughtered by bandits, and disenfranchised with the central

government, the peasant class was ripe for change.[69]

Mao once stated that, "the peasants are the sea, we are the fish, the sea is our habitat,"

meaning that in order to establish the first phase of his protracted framework he would have to

have a safe environment in which to begin his operations.[70] Mao would also look to villagers to

provide not only security but also provide the means in which his Red Army could sustain itself

in the hinterlands. In referencing the capabilities of the masses during one of his lectures Mao

suggests:

> [T]he support of the masses offers us great advantages as regards transport,
> assistance to wounded, intelligence, disruption of the enemy's position, etc. At the
> same time, the enemy can be put into an isolated position, thus further increasing our
> advantages. If, by misfortune, we are defeated, it will also be possible to escape or to
> find concealment.[71]

These are all key factors that would eventually enable Mao to build a force capable of conducting

a successful revolution.

One of the most basic means in which to influence a large base was through legitimacy.

An easy way to establish legitimacy is through creditability. Mao gained initial creditability by

---

[68]Zedong Mao, On Guerrilla Warfare: Tr. and with an Introduction by Samuel B. Griffith (New York: Praeger, 1961), 13.

[69]Ibid.,14

[70]Ibid.,13

[71]"Basic Tactics," How The Popular Masses Carry Out Military Action., accessed February 15, 2014, https://www.marxists.org/reference/archive/mao/selected-works/volume-6/mswv6_28.htm#ch1.

using his early life as a peasant in the Hunan province as a unifying factor. Being able to relate and understand the peasant population would give Mao an influencing advantage that the Nationalist couldn't match.

During the period of the 1920s, warlords ruled the rural area in China. The warlords were the law and their bands of militia were the enforcers. In order to financially support their murderous activities the warlords would seek compensation through the landlords. The landlords owned approximately 90% of the rural land in China and would extort an astonishing amount of taxes and rent from the local farmers and peasants who were already living at a subsistence level of means.

Though 15 plus years removed from this environment, Mao understood the effect that the warlords, the landlords, and the criminal gangs had on the rural population. One of the very first things Mao sought to do in order to establish legitimacy among the peasant population was to punish and dissolve the old system of rule in the rural areas and establish a new world order. Mao's Land reform program was a critical catalyst for his revolution. By removing the murderers and warlords and punishing the corrupt landlords, Mao was able to fill a void created by their demise. Through this theory of action Mao was able to create opportunity within the peasant population; an opportunity that Mao wouldn't let pass him by.

Just as Mao's understanding of the population was an enabler for popular support, the Nationalist's aggressive tactics further segregated the population from the government. The mid 1920s would see the initial split between KMT and Mao's CCP. This split would lead to an immediate eradication of 50,000 CCP communist party members. Looking to continue the communist purge, Chiang's KMT took to the hinterlands of Hunan and proceeded to round up and kill all sympathizers and suspected sympathizers, most of which came from the peasant population.[72] Overtime the estimated massacre of the countryside peasants in China was

---

[72]Jonathan Clements, *Mao* (London: Haus Pub., 2006), 48.

approximately over 300,000.[73]

Both the Nationalist and the CCP understood the power of the masses in rural regions but there was a fundamental difference in how each side would approach the population that was already tired and frustrated from decades of oppression at the hands of the warlords and landlords. Viewing the population as a sideshow and a nuisance, the Nationalist's approach towards the massive peasant class was heavy handed and often brutal in nature and over time the majority of the peasantry would side with the revolution. The Nationalist's approach of stick rather than carrot would ultimately favor the CCP and enable Mao to garner support through his influencing activities.

Looking to build on the initiative gained through his reputation, Mao was now poised to strengthen his bond with the population. Mao looked to strengthen this bond through his ability to influence the local villages and their small village governments with the use of accurate and applicable propaganda. The purpose of this was to expand the political party ideology and militarily arm the local peasantry with the means to resist the Nationalist's and their tactics. Looking to capitalize on the murderous mistakes that the Nationalist forces committed, Mao would use a strong propaganda campaign to influence and unite the masses.

Simply defined, propaganda is the information, ideas, or rumors deliberately spread widely to help or harm a person, group, movement, institution, or nation.[74] In the early years of the 1920s Mao would gain notoriety for his ability to organize labor unions in Hunan.[75] In addition to his organizational skills, Mao was also recognized for his early work as a writer and propagandist. During the early stages of the communist revolution Mao played a

---

[73]Jonathan Clements, *Mao* (London: Haus Pub., 2006), 74

[74]Merriam-Webster, *The Merriam Webster Dictionary* (Merriam Webster.), 'propaganda'.

[75]Rebecca E. Karl, *Mao Zedong and China in the Twentieth-century World: A Concise History* (Durham: Duke University Press, 2010), 22.

critical role in expanding the communist ideology through a series of newspaper articles. The narrative in which Mao used to garner support played to the needs and desires of his targeted population. Both Mao's organizational and propagandist skills would play an important role in rallying the peasant population.

Because Mao felt comfortable with the peasant population due to his upbringing the majority of Mao's influencing messages, or propaganda, would be in line with the peasant way of thought. Other times though, Mao knew that he might lack knowledge about the specific needs of some rural areas due to the diversity among the different villages and tribes. Understanding this dynamic, Mao would stress the importance to seek, understand, and address the specific grievances of each population base. Then, based on the findings, Mao would tailor his influencing messages to address the grievance. In a message to his followers Mao once stated:

> Correct leadership can only be developed on the principle of 'from the masses to the masses.' This means summing up the views of the masses, then taking the resulting ideas back to the masses, explaining and popularizing them until the masses embrace the ideas as their own.[76]

The messages that evolved from Mao's propaganda campaign during the early stages of the revolution were target specific and therefore accurate. In addition to the accuracy of the message they were also relevant based on timely and intimate knowledge of his base of support. But it was not just Mao's effective themes and messages that were key to his influencing the population, but also his delivery methods that would compliment his propaganda.[77]

Mao's understanding of the utility of his Red Army was very practical in nature. Mao did not see the army as purely militaristic in nature, but rather he sought to use his organization as a means to inform and influence the population. Mao states:

> The Red Army should not certainly confine itself to fighting; besides fighting to destroy

---

[76]Basic Tactics," Political Work., accessed February 22, 2014, https://www.marxists.org/reference/archive/mao/selected-works/volume-6/mswv6_28.htm#ch1.

[77]Ibid., ch1

the enemy's military strength, it should such important tasks as doing propaganda work among the massing, arming them, helping to establish revolutionary political power…the red army fight not merely for the sake of fighting, but in order to conduct propaganda work among the masses, organize them and arm them.[78]

Therefore in conjunction with the political ideology, Mao would use his forces to disseminate the CCP message. High illiteracy rates and the lack of basic communication tools like a radio were facts that would shape Mao's approach to the population. Understanding the capabilities of the peasant demographic, Mao preferred to use face-to-face and personal interaction as the vehicle to deliver the CCP propaganda.

In order for this message to not only reach the masses but also have some form of legitimacy the couriers would have to be viewed in a positive light by the peasantry. Therefore Mao put in place several principles and rules that would govern the action of the Red Army during their interactions with the peasant population in the rural areas. Mao's three rules of discipline and eight points of conduct would support his population centric line of effort.

The three rules were prompt obedience to orders, no confiscation of peasant property, and prompt delivery directly to authorities of all items confiscated from the landlords. The eight points were (1) replace all doors when you leave a house. (2) Return and roll up the straw matting on which you sleep. (3) Be courteous and polite to the people and help them when you can. (4) Return all borrowed articles. (5) Replace all damaged articles. (6) Be honest in all transactions with the peasants. (7) Pay for all articles purchased. (8) Be sanitary.[79]

The punishment for violation of the aforementioned rules was often swift and harsh. Mao understood the importance of having a delivery mechanism that would compliment his

---

[78]Basic Tactics," Political Work., https://www.marxists.org/reference/archive/mao/selected-works/volume-6/mswv6_28.htm#ch IV, (accessed February 22, 2014).

[79]John Ellis and John Ellis, *From the Barrel of a Gun: A History of Guerrilla, Revolutionary, and Counter-insurgency Warfare, from the Romans to the Present* (London: Greenhill Books, 1995), 189.

themes and messages. But beyond the obviousness of the reason for the three rules and eight points, Mao wanted to ensure that the conduct of the Red Army would continue to foster a positive relationship with the population that would look upon the Red Army as a legitimate and credible military force. In addition to a disciplined Red Army, Mao sought to empower every member of his force with the ability to effectively disseminate the party message. This approach would provide many vehicles in which Mao could reach the masses and deliver his message.

As mentioned several times throughout this section, Mao was very successful with gaining the support of the peasant population through his influence activities. His peasantry background lent itself well to understanding the operational environment. Mao's early career working for the communist party inside the urban areas also exposed him to the benefits of effectively developing propaganda themes and messages. Both his upbringing and his communist schooling were critical during the period in which Mao looked to rally the peasant population for a revolution. Mao's themes and messaging were accurate, applicable, and effective because of this. Through an accurate and aggressive propaganda campaign Mao was able to produce a message that resonated with the population.

Mao also intimately understood the capabilities of the peasant population. This understanding would drive his propaganda delivery approach. Looking to disseminate the most timely and accurate messages Mao would use his guerilla and later on, his conventional forces, to pass along the political ideology of the CCP. Mao's face-to-face approach was the most effective means due to high illiteracy rates but it also added a personal element to his relationship with the population.

CONCLUSION

The US Army is looking to conclude its 12-year war in Afghanistan. As the hostilities come to a close and the US Army enters an interwar period, there will be much discussion about how to best prepare for the next unknown adversary. There will be lessons learned and theories codified into doctrine. One of those topics of discussion that will be addressed is the approach on how to influence and gain the support of the population.

The US military's implementation of influencing operations through MISO in both Afghanistan and Iraq was aggressive. The framework for the development of themes and messages were operationally sound but the specific messages were not as effective as they could have been. The mechanism in which to deliver these aforementioned messages were also not as complimentary as they could have been. Pamphlet dropping and billboards posting are were not as effective as face-to-face using PYSOP Soldiers to influence a targeted audience.

Conversely, Mao and the CCP were very effective with their influencing campaign. The overarching themes developed were in line with the population and the specific messages addressed the peasant population's needs and wants. The accuracy and effectiveness of Mao's influencing themes and messages were a direct correlation to his intimate knowledge and understanding of the population in which he was trying to influence. Mao's peasant upbringing and exposure to the harsh realities of this lifestyle would be a source of great influencing potential. Mao's message dissemination techniques were complimentary toward his messages. Delivered through the Red Army, Mao understood the power of the face-to-face engagement with the population that he was seeking to gain support from.

Obviously there are many differences between 21st century Afghanistan and early 20th century China. One of the biggest differences that should be addressed in this monograph is the rival system. For the US Military, the rival system came in form of the insurgency in both Iraq and Afghanistan. This rival system has proven to be extremely adaptive and capable of learning how to effectively wage an insurgency. As for Mao's rival system, the Nationalist party was an enabler that often times appeared to lack the ability to learn and adapt to the dynamic environment. The inability to address the change would ultimately strengthen Mao and the CCP cause and be the downfall for the Nationalists.

Finally there have been many critical thoughts concerning how the US. Army conducted its influence operations. From the planning, developing, and dissemination it could be said that the US Army was not as effective as it could have been. As the Army moves to better itself and prepare for the next war there are some things that might improve the development and dissemination of messages in the future.

The first recommendation would address the relevancy and accuracy of the influencing themes and messages. Marketing from a business standpoint allows for a company to better provide a product for its target audience. Prior to placing a product on the shelf for sale, the most successful corporations will test a market to ensure the product is applicable and will sell. The development of themes and messages is a product that the PYSOP community provides and therefore the notion of testing a product through marketing is very applicable in this case.

The second recommendation addresses the message dissemination aspect of MISO. The US Army had the means to reach the desired target audience but often did not achieve the desired effectiveness that it sought. Based on the success that followed Mao in the early stages of the Chinese Revolutionary War, face-to-face engagement through a legitimate indigenous medium appears to achieve the greatest effect when dealing with a population. It is also understood that the availability of an indigenous medium is often not an option for many US Army forces operating among the population, which leads us to the third and final recommendation.

Mao capitalized on his influencing themes and messages through the use of his Red Army. Over time the Red Army gained legitimacy and also grew in size. Mao used this large vehicle to disseminate his messages and he never lacked the ability to reach the masses. As mentioned within this monograph, currently the US Army employs the PYSOP Soldier to conduct influence bidding. It takes time and a lot of resources to generate the capability that PYSOP Soldiers bring to the fight. Just as Mao had a large army that delivered the messages of the CCP, the US Army also many Soldiers in which to deliver the American message. Training and application of message dissemination that goes beyond the given talking points could be an effective approach to influencing and gaining the support of the population.

BIBLIOGRAPHY

"Basic Tactics." How The Popular Masses Carry Out Military Action. https://www.marxists.org/reference/archive/mao/selected-works/volume-6/mswv6_28.htm#ch1, (Accessed February 15, 2014.).

Beckett, I. F. W. *Modern Insurgencies and Counter-insurgencies: Guerrillas and Their Opponents since 1750.* London: Routledge, 2001.

Bianco, Lucien, and Muriel Bell. *Origins of the Chinese Revolution.* Stanford, CA: Stanford University Press, 1971.

Birtle, Andrew James. *US Army Counterinsurgency and Contingency Operations Doctrine, 1942-1976.* Washington, DC: Center of Military History, U.S. Army, 2006.

Bjorge, Gary J. *Moving the Enemy: Operational Art in the Chinese PLA's Huai Hai Campaign.* Fort Leavenworth, KS.: Combat Studies Institute Press, 2004.

Boorman, Scott A. *The Protracted Game; a Wei-ch'i Interpretation of Maoist Revolutionary Strategy.* New York: Oxford University Press, 1969.

"CIA World Factbook." CIA World Factbook. http://geography.about.com/library/cia/blcindex.htm. (Accessed February 25, 2014).

Clements, Jonathan. *Mao.* London: Haus Pub., 2006.

Cressy, Earl Herbert. *Understanding China; a Handbook of Background Information on Changing China.* New York: Nelson, 1957.

Elleman, Bruce A., and S. C. M. Paine. *Modern China: Continuity and Change 1644 to the Present.* Upper Saddle River, NJ: Prentice Hall, 2010.

Ellis, John, and John Ellis. *From the Barrel of a Gun: A History of Guerrilla, Revolutionary, and Counter-insurgency Warfare, from the Romans to the Present.* London: Greenhill Books, 1995.

Fitzgerald, C. P. *The Birth of Communist China.* New York: Praeger, 1966.

Galula, David. *Counterinsurgency Warfare; Theory and Practice.* New York: Praeger, 1964.

Grasso, June M., Jay P. Corrin, and Michael Kort. *Modernization and Revolution in China.* Armonk, NY: M. E. Sharpe, 1991.

Griffith, Samuel B. *Mao Tse-Tung on Guerrilla Warfare.* Praeger, 1961.

Hook, Brian, and Denis Crispin Twitchett. *The Cambridge Encyclopedia of China.* Cambridge: Cambridge University Press, 1991.

Hsü, Immanuel C. Y. *The Rise of Modern China*. New York: Oxford University Press, 1970.

Isaacs, Harold R. *The Tragedy of the Chinese Revolution*. Stanford, CA: Stanford University Press, 1961.

Joes, Anthony James. *Resisting Rebellion: The History and Politics of Counterinsurgency*. Lexington, KY: University Press of Kentucky, 2004.

Joes, Anthony James. *Victorious Insurgencies: Four Rebellions That Shaped Our World*. Lexington: University Press of Kentucky, 2010.

Johnson, Timothy D. *A Gallant Little Army: The Mexico City Campaign*. Lawrence, KS.: University Press of Kansas, 2007.

Karl, Rebecca E. *Mao Zedong and China in the Twentieth-century World: A Concise History*. Durham: Duke University Press, 2010.

Li, Xing. *The Rise of China and the Capitalist World Order*. Farnham, England: Ashgate Pub., 2010.

Mao, Zedong. *On Guerrilla Warfare: Tr.* and with an Introduction by Samuel B. Griffith. New York: Praeger, 1961.

Mao, Zedong, Stuart R. Schram, and Nancy Jane, Hodes. *Mao's Road to Power: Revolutionary Writings 1912-1949*. Armonk, NY: M. E. Sharpe, 1992.

"Mao's Stratagem of Land Reform." Global.. http://www.foreignaffairs.com/articles/70902/c-m-chang/maos-stratagem-of-land-reform?nocache=1, (Accessed February 8, 2014).

Merriam-Webster. *The Merriam Webster Dictionary*. Merriam Webster.

Munoz, Arturo. "U.S. Military Information Operations in Afghanistan." : Effectiveness of Psychological Operations 2001-2010.. http://www.rand.org/pubs/monographs/MG1060.html. (Accessed February 08, 2014).

O'Neill, Bard E. *Insurgency & Terrorism: From Revolution to Apocalypse*. Washington, DC: Potomac Books, 2005.

Psychological Operations. Washington, DC: Headquarters, Department of the Army, U.S. Marine Corps, 1993.

Rid, Thomas, and Thomas A. Keaney. *Understanding Counterinsurgency: Doctrine, Operations and Challenges*. Milton Park, Abingdon, Oxon,: Routledge, 2010.

Saich, Tony, and Bingzhang Yang. *The Rise to Power of the Chinese Communist Party: Documents and Analysis*. Armonk, NY: M. E. Sharpe, 1996.

Selden, Mark. *China in Revolution: The Yenan Way Revisited*. Armonk, NY: M. E. Sharpe, 1995.

Spence, Jonathan D. *Mao Zedong*. New York: Viking, 1999.

Tse-tsung, Chow. *The May Fourth Movement*. Harvard University Press, 1960.

Turabian, Kate L., John Grossman, and Alice Bennett. *A Manual for Writers of Term Papers, Theses, and Dissertations, 7th edition*. Chicago: University of Chicago Press, 1996.

Twitchett, Denis Crispin., and John King Fairbank. *The Cambridge History of China*. Cambridge: Cambridge University Press, 1978.

U.S. Army Information Proponent Office. "Instructor's Guide To Inform And Influence Activities." US Army War College. http://www.carlisle.army.mil/. (Accessed December 19, 2013).

The U.S. Army/Marine Corps Counterinsurgency Field Manual: U.S. Army Field Manual No. 3-24: Marine Corps Warfighting Publication No. 3-33.5. Chicago: University of Chicago Press, 2007.

Zhou, Cezong. *The May Fourth Movement: Intellectual Revolution in Modern China*. Cambridge: Harvard University Press, 1960.